# Optimize Your Resume

---

## DOs and DON'Ts the SamNova Way

### Ed Samuel

Copyright © 2019

All rights reserved. No part of this book may be reproduced, distributed or transmitted in anyway or form by any means, including imaging, copying, recording, writing or other methods without the prior written permission of the publisher.

For permission, please write to the publisher directly at address below:

Stonegate Publishing House
PO Box 501
Landenberg, PA   19350

Printed in the United States of America
ISBN: 9781694005724

#optimizingcareers
www.samnovainc.com

Book Editor and Design: Michele Chynoweth, Book Coach

# DEDICATION

*This journey and book are dedicated to
my three daughters, Jen, Trisha and Holly.*

## ACKNOWLEDGMENTS

I humble myself to God and Jesus Christ who guides and strengthens me in all that I do in HIS eyes.

My heartfelt thanks to Saradawn, my partner, wife and best friend of forty-two years for supporting me each step of the way with my business, this book, our family,
our walk with the Lord and so much more in my life.

A big shout out to Liz Brown, Be Well Life Coaching, Holly K. Sheridan, Esq., Trisha M Taylor, Jen Samuel and Saradawn Samuel for their review, advice
and feedback on this book.

# CONTENTS

|  | Introduction | 1 |
|---|---|---|
| Chapter 1 | What's Next? | 7 |
| Chapter 2 | Name, Location, Cell, Email and LinkedIn | 11 |
| Chapter 3 | Title | 15 |
| Chapter 4 | Profile Summary | 19 |
| Chapter 5 | Core Competencies | 25 |
| Chapter 6 | Key Accomplishments and Value Proposition | 29 |
| Chapter 7 | Firm/Organization, Employment and Timeframes | 39 |
| Chapter 8 | Job Titles, Responsibilities and Accomplishments | 43 |
| Chapter 9 | Early Career | 51 |
| Chapter 10 | Education and Certifications | 55 |
| Chapter 11 | Awards | 61 |
| Chapter 12 | Professional Development | 65 |
| Chapter 13 | Technical Skills | 69 |
| Chapter 14 | Presentations and Publications | 73 |
| Chapter 15 | Patents | 75 |
| Chapter 16 | Professional Organizations | 81 |
| Chapter 17 | Volunteer and Community | 85 |
| Chapter 18 | Standards – Look, Feel and Length | 89 |
| Chapter 19 | Resume Sections and Template | 93 |
| Chapter 20 | Ultimate DOs and DON'Ts | 99 |
|  | Resources and Obtaining a Word Resume Template | 101 |

# FOREWORD
## by Joe "Doc" Dougherty

Think about this. When we get sick, we visit a doctor. When we struggle with taxes, we seek the advice of a good tax accountant. When a sticky legal matter develops, we turn to a good lawyer. When we experience car troubles, we ask a good car mechanic to get us back on the road. When there are leaks in the kitchen or bathroom we lean on a good plumber. We insist on good doctors, good accountants, good lawyers, good mechanics, good plumbers. We demand experts!

Why then, for something as important as our own careers, do we believe that we can do it our self and/or seek advice from family and friends?

A resume is pretty darn important don't you think? Sure, good resumes tell a story, get leaders excited, sell our qualifications, get us good interviews with good companies, and get us solid compensation packages that we deserve allowing us to provide for ourselves and our loved ones. And yet most people don't seek out the same expertise on which we insist with other critical points of our day-to-day lives.

Ed Samuel is an expert. He has proven himself time and time again in this very complex job market. He is trusted—he asks tough questions, he delivers and he helps candidates get the best offers at the best companies.

Optimizing Your Resume

He knows how important resumes are, providing first impressions, strong highlights, quantifiable accomplishments, delivering great outcomes, in the few seconds that each leader may initially spend reviewing a resume.

Consider Ed's own portfolio of work. He is a successful entrepreneur, industry speaker, executive recruiter, general manager, accomplished career consultant and more.

Ed delivered strong talent for a sixty-year-old "Best Place to Work" international firm whose employees generated over 5,000 patents over the years. He was a senior executive career consultant for one of the most prestigious career management firms on the east coast.

He understands that resumes serve one purpose only: to get you phone screened and/or interviewed. He believes that the three most important factors for good resumes are packaging, packaging and packaging.

Ed is as honest as they come. He truly cares. The thousands of people he has assisted throughout his career will tell you much better than I can. Ed Samuel makes a difference-a huge difference! He helps to deliver great outcomes vis-a-vis landing a good job. Most of those whom he has helped will tell you they landed good jobs, and many were promoted in a short time.

Ed has taken the time to package so much of his great advice for all to review in this outstanding book. Why wouldn't you want to read about essential tips and must-haves from one of the outstanding career coaches of our time?

Do NOT Go About This Yourself! Do NOT depend on well-intended family members and friends who want to help with your resume. They can help in other ways.

Listen to Ed and read this book. You will deliver a better product to a tough marketplace that demands only the "best of the best!"

---

Foreword Author – Joe "Doc" Dougherty

Joe Dougherty, or Joe "Doc" as he is known by many, is one of the pre-eminent career coaches and experts in the marketplace today. Joe is an accomplished career coach, executive search leader, entrepreneur, HR Consulting Leader and more.

He helped to grow a financial services firm from 300 to 3,000+ employees during his watch.

He was a key architect in the growth of a two-person startup career management firm and ultimately grew that business to where the company is today recognized as the largest privately held human capital consulting and career management firm in the Mid-Atlantic region. Before he sold his interest early in 2019, the firm had delivered consulting work to close to 4,000 corporate clients in the region.

Today Joe has started his third business, Joe Doc Consulting (joedocconsulting.com) and is delivering private career coaching and recruiting services to selected organizations.

Optimizing Your Resume

# INTRODUCTION

*"You just can't beat the person who never gives up."*
Babe Ruth

I decided to write *Optimize Your Resume—DOs and DON'Ts the SamNova Way* to help more people advance in their careers than my team or I could ever help individually. I have reviewed no less than 3,000 resumes in multiple capacities; as a hiring manager across many roles and industries, recruiter, retained search consultant, corporate recruiting leader and as a career coach.

I contend the vast majority (97%) of resumes could be written far better with a pronounced boldness in articulating a person's story and true value proposition. This point holds true not just for C-level executives but for everyone: vice presidents, directors, managers, supervisors, individual contributors, teachers and hourly workers.

One of the challenges with writing resumes is that everyone has an opinion and/or gives advice as to what should and should not be on a resume. Some of the advice is sound, much of the advice sounds good and some is simply dead wrong.

# Optimizing Your Resume

Many resume writers and outplacement firm transition coaches will suggest changes to format, provide feedback on word use and add new sections if needed. But they spend way too much time worrying about keeping a resume to only two pages. Their other concern is that, due to very limited time constraints, they simply cannot and will not invest the needed time with their clients to get it right in all ways. Another challenge is that unless the resume writer has deep cross-industry real-life experience, they have a very limited ability to challenge content.

When we meet with clients to write or rewrite their resumes it's never about format as much as the depth and quality of the value proposition and competencies. We are relentless in finding a person's greatest tangible value and contributions. I do not support rushing a resume but dissecting it part by part and challenging every word and every piece of content.

We have been known to invest more than six hours on a resume and will do whatever it takes to get it right. I unfortunately have witnessed just the opposite with many people telling us, "I did get resume help. I hired a resume writer/career coach and I'm still not getting interviews or landing a job." We then meet with the client and review his or her resume and what has been done to date. What we find is that the client's resume has had some improvement based on feedback from friends, recruiters, outplacement transition coaches and even the lower cost $99 resume writers. We ask the question, "how much time did they spend with you on your resume?" The answer we commonly get back is, "thirty minutes to an hour." In many cases, it comes down to a time clock and speed. Our approach is very different as the first meeting alone may last two hours as a starting point. We will revamp the entire resume based on our standards, word for word, until we are certain the very best of a person's value proposition and competencies come forth.

For those who have lost their jobs, there tends to be an immediate push to get the resume updated and out ASAP. But not as much focus is placed on stepping back and re-evaluating the entire resume top to bottom. I have even seen outplacement firms, resume writers and coaches assist in this speed exercise mainly due to how they are paid. The reality is that a price is paid when a resume is rushed into the job marketplace without making it the very best presentation of a person's value proposition. This is especially true when not capturing correctly the value proposition of the most recent job held. Many times, we hear clients complain that they literally applied to fifty to one hundred jobs in a sixty-day period using a quickly updated resume and not gotten a single interview. It's simply because the resume was not strong.

Our approach has been, let's slow down, spend seven-plus days until we get it right and then start targeting the resume to the right firms and decision makers. Often, when you finally get your resume to a potential decision maker or hiring manger, you only have one shot at getting his or her attention, not two to three shots to garner interest. This is why I'm a big believer of getting it right the first time even if it takes more time to get a quality resume completed.

When I led a large corporate recruiting team for a billion-dollar medical device division, my recruiters would on average have seven seconds to review a resume and decide if it was worth going any further. Let's face it, that is not a lot of time. I am proof positive that if the first page of your resume is not a homerun, you have put yourself in a deep hole and out of contention. It is a crime when that happens, especially when the best of you is on page two of your resume and the decision maker decided not to flip to that page.

## Optimizing Your Resume

One of the best examples I can give you is the story of a manager with thirty years of experience who found himself unemployed after being with one firm his entire career. He had applied to too many firms in his first three to four months, using a resume he had created with advice received from others including an outplacement transition consultant. He was getting no interviews at all. He then heard about SamNova and decided to contact us for help.

I remember meeting with him two to three times until we were able to craft a night and day version of his story and valuation proposition on his new resume. Once we were done, I asked him to go back and replace his old resume with the new one at each of the firms he had applied to over the previous months. Within a day or two, he received a phone call from a senior leader at a firm. The Vice President said, "I want to meet with you ASAP since anyone who could transform and improve his resume like you did is a person I want working here at my firm." The short of this story is that my client interviewed and was subsequently hired—all due to the optimization of his resume.

Also, I really want this book to help fix many common mistakes I see on resumes every day. These mistakes include the following:

- spelling errors
- inconsistencies
- wrong font size
- no title or poor title
- bold words
- too much fluff
- wrong alignment
- too wordy
- dense wording
- no tangible and quantifiable accomplishments

- not speaking to breadth and scope
- being known for everything
- creating a list centric resume
- using words such as numerous, many, a few, some
- suppressing years of experience
- forcing resume to 1 to 2 pages
- leaving out volunteer work
- using etc. instead of calling out a few of the most important areas
- stating you were recruited out of a firm
- having gaps or unaccounted time periods
- not making a compelling argument of your value proposition on first page of resume

This is not the entire list of mistakes but a good handful of them that this book will address.

This book can be applied in total or in part to virtually all careers. It can also help young adults leaving college, vocational tech school or high school and looking for his or her very first or second job.

Although I do not touch on every conceivable resume situation for all jobs across all industries, I do believe that 90% of the principals I cover can be applied to virtually any resume. I also realize it's not an exact cookie cutter for every single person and situation, but exceptions should be rare. I hope and trust that if you follow each chapter of my book, it will force you to slow down and re-think what and how you are stating something and do so with your eyes and ears wide open.

I hope you not only enjoy this book but find it a practical step by step guide in writing, revamping or improving your resume. The aim is to bring out the very best of who you are and your contributions to organizations and/or firms that you have supported in the workplace.

Optimizing Your Resume

A great resume will improve your self-confidence, increase your market value, garner more interest about you and provide you a platform to optimize your career.

# Chapter 1
## What's Next?

*"The purposes of a person's heart are deep waters, but one who has insight draws them out."*
Proverbs 20:5

Before they begin writing a resume, the first thing I ask my clients is this question: "What do you want to do next in your career and life?" I want to be certain you know where you're headed before we jump to writing or updating your resume. If you are dead certain you love your career and want to stay in that field, wonderful, then we can get started right away.

If you are in a personal struggle and truly believe you must stay in your career and job no matter what, that's another reason to begin work on your resume right away. Unfortunately, I've had endless situations of moms who need immediate help with their resumes because their husbands walked out on them and their young children. In these situations, the mom needs her resume done ASAP and getting any job will suffice. Their goal of taking care of their children trumps worrying about moving into an ideal career or job.

If you are certain you know what you want to do next, or must do next, then proceed to Chapter 3 now. If not, and it took you more than three to four seconds to answer the above question, "What do you want to do next in your career and life?" then please continue reading.

Believe it or not, when I ask my clients, "What do you want to do next?" 85% will quickly say, "I just don't know" or take a very long ten seconds plus and answer with a weak, "I think so." At that point, we need to dig deeper and slow the resume process down since we literally are not sure where we are headed. Sometimes clients have even done their own assessing and they know in their guts it's time to shift their careers or at a minimum explore all the other options out there. In these cases, we jump into a new line of discussion to help.

My strong preference when trying to determine what to do next if unsure is to conduct a comprehensive career assessment and consultation with an experienced consultant. Fees for the assessments and consultations we offer range from a low of $180 to a high of $475 depending on the consultant assigned to work with you. Our fees are below market since the tool we use is underwritten by a non-profit as compared to other tools that can cost twice as much or more.

Our proven assessment tool goes deep into personality, interests, skills and values. The assessment includes a twenty-four-page summary report and we will spend upwards of two hours reviewing it with a client. Our tool will evaluate more than ninety-five career areas. Our goal is to try to narrow down one to three areas of consideration for a career focus. Then, we strongly encourage you to pray about these results and discuss them with your loved ones, friends, mentors or parents before making a final decision. Once you land on a career direction, it's time to focus on Chapter 3 of this book.

Unfortunately, many times a resume writer, career coach and especially an outplacement firm will avoid asking you, "What do you want to do next?" The reason is that they are, for the most part, on the clock and are not getting paid by an employer or you directly to do a full-blown assessment and consultation. My experience is most people want or need to take an assessment of some kind or at a minimum want to validate their current direction.

I was coaching a CFO a few years for a Fortune 500 firm and asked him, "What do you want to do next?" He said, "I love being a CFO and my career in finance, BUT Ed, I want to do an assessment with you to validate that I'm not missing anything else that I could potentially be doing in my life and career. I don't want to look back twenty years from now and say, I wish I knew, or I might have been this or that." So, even in this case, when people say they think they want to stay in their careers but have a slight question mark about what else may be out there, an assessment and consultation can help validate that they are best suited to staying in their career fields.

As a man of faith, I believe we are all created uniquely for a reason and that we have an opportunity to be the very best we can be in this lifetime. When you are focused in a career that truly inspires and brings out the best of you, it affords you a greater probability of being happier at work. You may also have a much greater positive impact on others.

---

## Principles – What's Next?

1. Ask yourself the question, "What do I want to do next?"

2. If you are certain as to your direction, validate that decision by doing a career assessment.

3. Don't let a resume writer or coach pressure you to move quickly to update your resume if you are not sure what you want to do next – slow it down.

4. Find a career assessment consultant who can help you find the best answer for your future. Be sure all assessments include four parts: Personality, Interests, Skills and Values, and that you are working with a certified career assessment consultant endorsed by the International Coaching Federation.

5. Inquire at SamNova, Inc. to help you do an assessment and consultation.

# Chapter 2
## Name, Location, Cell, Email and LinkedIn

*"Make your resume John Deere strong."*
Ed Samuel

First things first. Put your name, location, cell number, email address and LinkedIn URL at the top of your resume.

The look and feel should be as follows:

# Ed Samuel, CPA

Greater Denver, CO
492-910-0010    linkedin.com/in/edsamuel/    esamuel@samnovainc.com

---

**NAME:** Always put your name in a larger font size and in bold so it stands out. We recommend Cambria 22 as a minimum. Many times, I see resumes with small font sizes and it's hard to quickly garner the name. Make it very easy and quick to spot your name.

# Optimizing Your Resume

Put your name in **BOLD** and let people know who you are and make no bones about it. If you have an active certification, then you have the option to add it after your name. The example above indicates Ed Samuel holds an active CPA license. If a certificate is inactive, it would be inappropriate to list it after your name. Examples of other designations include PMP, CFP, CMA, CISA, CSCP and many more.

**LOCATION:** Yes, location does matter. Not having one or writing United States is never advised. The reason is that the decision maker or recruiter wants to know where you live today—it's that simple. When a location is missing, the immediate question arises, why are you hiding where you live? It conjures up the question, what else are you hiding on your resume? It creates frustration and it's never positive. The other area of location that can be a problem is putting down the town you live in when the average person has no idea where it might be located in the state. You are far better off to insert Greater Phoenix, AZ or Greater Boston, MA, etc.

A common mistake made is listing your private street address or apartment number on the resume. It is absolutely NOT needed or required when sending your resume to a decision maker. No one needs to map you to the precise location and home where you live to decide if they are going to interview or hire you. Your home address is confidential and privileged information.

The larger concern with social media and the internet is that your resume could get into the hands of too many bad people. All you need to put down is Greater Miami, FL or Greater Fort Myers, FL but not your street address or apartment number. Once you formally apply for a job at a firm or organization, you will be asked on their system or hard copy paperwork to enter your home address information. But, at that point, the company or organization you applied to has the responsibility to protect your private information in their database or filing system.

**CELL NUMBER:** Always list your cell number – never your home phone. If you want to garner support and consideration quickly, allow hiring managers and recruiters to get to you quickly. Nobody wants to call your home number and hear, "the Smiths can't come to the phone now, please leave a message" and hear the family dog barking in the background. It is equally frustrating when a spouse or significant other answers and must relay the message. All of this adds to a recruiter's frustration and is not positive.

**LINKEDIN:** Always add your public LinkedIn URL. If you don't have a LinkedIn profile, get one or ask someone to create one for you. You will also have the option to edit your public LinkedIn URL and eliminate a system generated one that adds many numbers to the end. Here's an example:

Unedited URL: **www.linkedin/in/edsamuel2558603-30**
Edited URL: www.linkedin/in/edsamuel1
(Try to keep your URL as short as possible.)

Research has shown that between 70% to 85% of recruiters and hiring managers source and/or validate potential candidates using LinkedIn. The number is simply too high to ignore, and you need to have a robust and full profile. Leaving it off the resume may also tell a potential employer that you are "not current" or set in your ways. It's not good and it will be perceived way more negatively than positively by recruiters or potential hiring managers.

**EMAIL:** Make it easy for people to contact you by listing your email at the top of your resume. I've seen cases where a resume is missing an email and even in some cases a phone number. There is a school of thought to get a newer email to demonstrate that you are current. Emails such as AOL, Hotmail, Yahoo can date you as "old." I have mixed feelings on this issue since your value proposition on your resume should always trump any concern about using an old email address. But, beyond that concern, never use an over the top email that you set up for fun years ago. Example, wildnwetpaul@hotmail.com or imaygonuts@aol.com. These types of emails are unacceptable and although innocent at one level, they give a far more negative impression about your professionalism. If needed, simply create a new email on Outlook or Gmail and use it in all aspects of your job search.

## Principles - Name, Location, Cell, Email and LinkedIn

1. **Make your name stand out with a larger font.**

2. **Never list an unfamiliar town – err on using Greater (city, state).**

3. **Never put the street address or apartment number on a resume.**

4. **List your cell number and make it easy for people to reach you quickly.**

5. **Add your customized LinkedIn URL.**

6. **Replace odd or far out emails with a mainstream one.**

# Chapter 3
# Title

*"The future belongs to those who believe in the beauty of their dreams."*
Eleanor Roosevelt

One of the most important aspects of a resume is to ensure your title accurately defines who you are in the marketplace. The title should stand out at the top of a resume. I recommend Cambria font size 18. Unfortunately, more than 35% of all resumes I review lack a clear title at the top of the resume. I understand why people may be reluctant to declare a title, especially when someone can do many things. It's even natural to not want to pin yourself down to a singular title. On the other hand, it's a big problem for a recruiter or decision maker trying to figure who you are and how you may possibly fit into a job or organization he or she has in mind.

When it comes to recruiters, there are only two kinds: those who are fast and efficient, and those who are slow and lazy. In both cases, when a resume crosses their desks and has no title, it creates frustration. As a former recruiter for years, I promise you it creates negative energy since you want the reader to somehow figure out who you are and your place in the marketplace.

In addition, please avoid making a title so general that it still begs the question, "Who are you?"

Example of what **NOT** to do:

### Financial Professional

This could mean just about anything within finance ranks. Are you in financial services, financial analysis, accounting, compliance? And on it goes. If you are in Financial Services as an example, are you in risk management, an advisor, portfolio manager, relationship manager, trader? Again, you put the onus on the reader to somehow analyze your resume and try to figure out just who you are. I've seen this done many times across all functions and industries such as IT Professional, Finance Executive, Supply Chain Professional, and the list goes on and on. Remember, you have on average about seven seconds for a recruiter or hiring manager to make a decision about you at the first glance of your resume. You don't want to waste all of that seven seconds with them trying to figure out who you are.

Your title should be reflective of the types of positions you recently held. Let's look at an example of a person who has a Risk Management background.

Most recent role: Risk Director for 4 years
Previous role: Senior Risk Director for 10 years
Previous role: Senior Risk Manager 5 years

In this case, I could make an argument that the title of Senior Risk Director could be a good one to use. One could also use the title of Risk Director as being an even better choice. The reason why is that Risk Director gives you the flexibility of upward movement to a Senior Risk Director role and downward movement to a Senior Risk Manager role or to remain at Risk Director. I prefer flexibility in a title whenever possible.

Example of what TO do:

**Senior Risk Director**

Let's stay with this example and give it another twist. If a person decides to use Senior Risk Director, he or she still has the flexibility to move upward to a Vice President role and downward to a Director role but may end up not being favorably viewed for a Risk Manager level role any longer.

Let's look at another example with more focus on breadth, scope of work and targeting your next job. If you're a CEO for a $100M firm and you want to advance your career, you may not want to put CEO as your title on your resume. You may want to use Senior Vice President or Chief Operating Officer. The reason is that if you are pursuing $10B firms, you will most likely be at Vice President level and not the CEO level.

Here is another example. You're a Senior Accountant and in the last two jobs, you were also a Senior Accountant. You are perfectly content and happy in this role and want to continue to be a Senior Accountant. In that case, it's simple; put Senior Accountant at the top of your resume.

The other reason title becomes so important is that it brings your next job into focus and it becomes more targeted. The more targeted you can become in your thinking with a strong focused title on your resume, the more success you will enjoy in getting to where you want to go next.

I believe a job title is so important that if you told me it took several hours on your own or with a resume writer or career coach to discuss it, I'd tell you "time well spent." A few hours invested on this question could shave off weeks and months in your job search. Please be very careful of resume writers or career coaches who want to push you quickly to pick a title without careful consideration and discussion.

## Principles – Title

1. **Never leave the title area blank and force people to figure out who you are.**

2. **Make it easy for decision makers to know who you are and do not put the onus on them to figure it out.**

3. **Create flexibility to give yourself upward, downward or lateral mobility.**

4. **Factor in the breadth, scope and title of your next job.**

5. **Think it through and don't feel pressured or rushed on declaring a job title.**

# Chapter 4
## **Profile Summary**

*"Being a role model is the most powerful form of educating."*
John Wooden

At the beginning of every resume under the title should be a crisp focused summary as to who you are, what you are good at and something that makes you unique. I like to call this summary your traditional "elevator pitch." It's when you get into an elevator with a President of a firm and he or she asks you, "What do you do for a living?" It's intended to be no more than a thirty-second pitch so when the elevator stops on the fortieth floor, the president knows enough about you and hopefully you generated enough interest for he or she to ask for your personal business card.

The profile section needs to be broken into three unique sections as follows:

a. A sentence that explains your title, years of experience and the industries you have supported.
b. The depth of expertise you bring forward.
c. Two traits that you are known for.

Let's break these sections down and explain how to construct each one.

## Optimizing Your Resume

I'll use a Marketing Manager as an example. Below is how I recommend the <u>first</u> sentence be written:

**A senior marketing manager with more than 20 years of experience supporting $1B pharmaceutical firms.**

This sentence is concise and gets to the point quickly. By stating the years of experience, the reader knows immediately your depth and if you are in your early, mid or later career.

I am also never one to run scared on resumes. I don't want you to think if you have more than 25 years listed, you're old and will never be considered for a new job opportunity. I realize there are a group of resume writers and coaches who believe you should mask certain key information like years of experience in a way that tries to trick the decision maker into thinking you are far younger. I understand and deal with the age bias concern all the time. My argument against this logic is that when the employer, hiring manager or recruiter finally asks enough questions and/or finally meets you, the bias does not go away. If anything, once it's discovered, you have now layered on a concern with what might be viewed as a lack of integrity since you were not honest. From a coaching standpoint, I also don't want my clients wasting their time or an employer's time when it can be better spent working with people who don't have a bias.

The other argument is that when someone reads your resume and you force him or her to try to figure out the depth of your experience, it's far more a negative than a positive. I know some recruiters who will simply put your resume in the NO GO pile as their instincts are telling them "this person is hiding things and I don't have time to do detective work at my expense."

When it comes to expertise, the key to this section of the profile is to focus in on the heart of what you are good at and have depth in. It's not intended to be everything that you know as much as a solid chunk of the best competencies and experience you have at this point in your career. Below is how I recommend the second sentence be written:

**Expertise includes strategic planning, new product development, competitive analysis, digital marketing, agency collaboration, print ads, blogging, campaign management and voice of the customer.**

Be sure to also put your expertise in order of priority. In this example, strategic planning is the highest followed by new product development. Never put these areas of expertise randomly, please be thoughtful. Again, it's not a statement intended to list everything that you do or know. At most, this should be two-and-a-half lines at most.

Below is how I recommend the third or final sentence be written:

**Known for growing market share and building high performing teams.**

At the end of the summary section clearly state two traits for which you are known. I've seen a lot of resumes that list far too many outstanding qualities—a dozen or more in fact.

If you are known for everything, you really are known for nothing. I've asked many candidates this question, "What are two things you are known for?" Surprisingly, most people cannot tell me outright. That's a problem and not just for the resume. What if you were asked the same question during an interview? I often suggest to my clients that they talk to three

# Optimizing Your Resume

or four of their references and ask them that same question. Look for themes across the board to help you isolate two key traits that depict what differentiates you from others.

Let's look at what a complete Profile Summary looks like when it all comes together:

**A senior marketing manager with more than 20 years of experience supporting $1B pharmaceutical firms. Expertise includes strategic planning, product development, competitive analysis, digital marketing, agency collaboration, print ads, blogging campaign management and voice of the customer. Known for growing new market share and building high performing teams.**

Once you go beyond five lines on your profile, it stops being a crisp snapshot of who you are, and it begins to look and feel wordy. I've seen many summaries with eight lines or more including words that add little to no value. It also comes across as running scared since you seem to have to say every little detail about who you are at length and lack the ability to provide a lean and concise summary.

The other big mistake made is that people insert words in the summary section that **add little to no value.** These words include:

- highly energetic
- solid team player
- effective listener
- results oriented
- highly motivated
- driven
- people person
- excellent, outstanding, focused, noteworthy
- successful

All of these words are "fluff" and will not awe the recruiter or decision maker. In fact, Applicant Tracking System (ATS) screening systems have a fluff meter and your resume hit rate will drop much lower with the use of all the fluff words. This means your resume will not come out the other end as a viable candidate for the posted position.

If anything, you are filling space on the resume and overreaching in promoting yourself. The other question that arises when you are using words like, "I am excellent" at this or that in any one area is, "does that mean you are less than excellent at other areas?" Use the logic that you are excellent or outstanding at everything that's listed on your resume. In this same line of thinking, don't use the word "successful." Everything on your resume should be successful and not call out one or two areas more so than others.

Another common mistake in the profile section is to mix several accomplishments in with who you are and make it a hodge-podge of information. It will almost always push the length beyond my five-line limit.

Finally, keep the summary profile to no more than five lines in total including all three parts. It will force you to prioritize what you are truly good at when describing yourself. This type of profile summary can then be used as the traditional elevator pitch. If you were to step in an elevator with a decision maker and he or she were to simply ask, "What do you do?" this type of profile summary can be used to answer the question in those thirty seconds or so and hopefully lead the person to ask for your business card.

---

## Principles – Profile Summary

1. Keep the profile to no more than five lines but no less than four lines for the first twenty years on your resume.

2. Always state your approximate years of experience.

3. State the industries you supported.

4. Focus on the heart of your expertise – not every single thing you know.

5. Ask your references if unsure the two traits for which you are best known.

6. Avoid at all costs adding "fluff" or unneeded words.

# Chapter 5
# Core Competencies

*"Opportunities don't happen. You create them."*
Chris Grosser

An important part of a resume pertains to you declaring what core business competencies you will bring forward to a new job. I want you to think about the top nine competencies at which you are very skilled. Do NOT automatically use the skills that people have endorsed you for on LinkedIn. This is your own list of deep expertise that you possess.

I suggest you think about it like Olympic scoring. Look at your depth of competencies and ask yourself, am I a 10.0 or a 9.5 or 9.8. What we are looking for are only the 10.0s.

If we stay with the Marketing example in Chapter 4, below is what you can use as an example and model:

### Core Competencies

| | | |
|---|---|---|
| Strategic Planning | Voice of the Customer | Direct Mail |
| New Products | High Performing Teams | Ad Agencies |
| Branding | Competitive Analysis | Social Media |

## Optimizing Your Resume

I am perfectly fine if you want to duplicate any of the expertise you called out in your Profile Summary on this list. This list is intended to make a bold statement again on your expertise, deep experience and skills.

Please avoid adding soft skills or traits such as: Results Oriented, Team Player, Effective Manager.

If you are a financial advisor, IT developer, compliance officer and such that require a certain level of certification, you can use one or more of them as one of your core competencies. Here is an example pertaining to a financial advisor:

**- Series 7, 63**

Another way to rationalize these nine competencies is to assume you were hired at a firm. After five months on the job, you walk into your manager's office and say, "We need to hire a consultant to do Branding." That would not be good since you declared on your resume you had deep Branding experience and it was one of your core competencies. Your new boss would not be so pleased if you said you possessed deep expertise and then turned around and said you really didn't and you needed to hire a consultant now. That could get you into some trouble.

But I also want you to stay away from making a long list. I've seen resumes that have eighteen or more competencies listed—literally. Not good. When you do such, it really hurts how you are viewed. A recruiter or hiring manager may view a long list as someone trying to say he or she has expertise in everything which usually means that person has expertise in nothing. It can also be viewed as a person who is running scared on his or her resume and feeling like he or she has to cover every single area versus rising up and stating, "I'm really good in these key areas." Decision makers like candidates that can elevate themselves to a higher level using a more concise and focused approach. Most decision makers realize that you're good at many things and you are not expected to list everything you know. Please keep it to nine key competencies.

One final point on building your competencies— do not list them randomly. Make the first column three of your very best competencies. A reader will look at the beginning of any section on your resume at a quick glance, so be sure the best of the best appears first. They may not even focus on the second two columns.

---

## Principles – Core Competencies

1. **Keep your list to no more than nine competencies in which you would receive 10.0 scores only.**

2. **Stay away from any fluff or only stating soft skills.**

3. **It's perfectly fine to duplicate expertise from your summary profile as one or more of your core competencies.**

4. **Be sure the first column represents the best of the best of your competencies.**

Optimizing Your Resume

# Chapter 6
# Key Accomplishments and Value Proposition

*"Perfection is not attainable, but if we chase perfection, we can catch excellence."*
Vince Lombardi

Your value proposition and key accomplishments are without a doubt, the most important parts of any resume. You get this right, you get a lot right—everything from how you are perceived, garnering attention in that first seven seconds by a decision maker, to validating your market value by the reader. It's imperative that you call out your key accomplishments on the first page of your resume. This applies to virtually everyone except those leaving school or college and entering the workforce for the first time.

I am a stickler for isolating your biggest five accomplishments which I'll refer to as the **Big 5.** These accomplishments represent the greatest value you have had at a firm or organization in your work history; whether you have been at it for two years or thirty-five years.

One way of thinking about creating the **Big 5** is to imagine going into an interview with the owner of a firm. After you exchange introductions, the owner says to you, "I've glanced over your resume and here's what I want to know: What are your greatest claims to fame where you had the biggest tangible impact in the workplace? We have about forty-five minutes left and you can start now." What would you say? What you better say is exactly what you're being asked to say. Having these **Big 5** accomplishments will help you immediately focus on answering that question.

Here is a sample list of questions I want you to ask yourself to help jog your memory. This is the same list of questions you need to ask yourself for each position you have held in your career.

a. How much did you produce in a given month, quarter or year?
b. How many customers did you service each day, week, month or year?
c. What was the biggest initiative you led? What did it result in?
d. What was the largest costs savings you achieved?
e. How much new market share did you gain?
f. What products did you increase margin for?
g. How much did you improve cash flow by?
h. What was your top line sales number over the last five years?
i. How many projects did you manage? Were they within budget and on time?
j. What was the largest risk mitigation effort you led?
k. When did you receive the biggest recognition and for what?
l. If you won awards, what did you do to achieve them?
m. How many audits did you pass?
n. How many new product launches did you lead and what was the revenue impact?

o. How many experiments did you do this year?
p. What was your biggest and most challenging project?
q. What was the biggest client or customer issue that you resolved?
r. What was the productivity of the new software solution impacting the entire testing team?
s. What was the average DSO over the last five years?
t. Can you connect yourself to anything the firm or organization achieved that you were "pivotal" to?
u. How many mergers and acquisitions did you lead?
v. How many training classes did you hold?
w. What was the employee retention rate over last five years?
x. How many injuries were reported at the plant? Did accidents decrease under your watch?
y. What was the decrease in customer returns?
z. How many fraud transactions were caught this past year?

This list of questions will get you thinking in a more concrete way about your accomplishments. Tangible and quantifiable accomplishments are the best way to articulate your value proposition. Stating that you did an activity without a noted or understood outcome simply puts you in a less favorable position when going up against others who can. Tangible accomplishments will have some form of the following:

- $1K, $10K $100K, $1M, $10M+
- % improvement
- Hard score – such as a customer satisfaction score of 9.9/10.0
- Days Sales Outstanding or DSO
- ROI/ROA improvement %

# Optimizing Your Resume

One of the challenges my clients will often tell me is, "Ed, I can't remember." That's understandable at one level. At another, every time you work for a firm or organization and you DO NOT track and measure your performance, you put yourself in this awkward position when it comes time to answer these types of questions. These questions again are getting at your true value proposition. Remember, a statement that has no value attached to it is simply an activity. I contest that a company or recruiter will be far more interested in you if you can state with confidence your value.

If you are not sure of what you did, then it's time to create what I call a "guestimate." It is a very conservative way to quantify something that you did. As a former CFO it may come natural to me, but you don't have to be a CFO to use logic to get to a reasonable result.

Let's use an example of a Learning and Development Manager that taught classes fifteen years ago for a firm for seven years. No records or metrics were kept, no monthly reports. We begin by asking these questions: "How many classes did you teach a year? Was it one or was it one hundred?" Most people will say it was certainly more than one. I'll then dig deeper with another question: "How many did you average per month?" I'll get an answer back. "Well, Ed it was about one a month." Great, we now have a rough answer. This person taught twelve classes a year. Done. Use this same logic if you are struggling in quantifying anything. The ONLY caution when doing so is to always be conservative and not exaggerate or make up numbers but be in striking range of an honest guestimate. If you simply make up a number and get in front of a very sharp CFO or hiring manager, you don't want them to back you into any kind of a corner and then all agree that the number is way off. That then kills the credibility of not just that accomplishment but perhaps your entire resume. So, for every number, $ or % you have on a resume, just be prepared to explain how you came up with it.

Let's now look at the structure of an accomplishment sentence on a resume. It's perfectly fine to have a one-line accomplishment and even make it two lines. But, NEVER make an accomplishment three lines. Every time you do so, it's because you want to explain how you did it, why you did and everyone that was impacted by it. That's not the purpose of a resume. You job is to explain what you did and what it resulted in and IF you want to elaborate, do so with ONLY a FEW words.

I want your accomplishments to have the following two core components:

**What did you do? and What did it Result in? (quantified)**

Let's look at a few examples:

Example 1: Led team that **implemented Oracle ERP** system and **saved firm $11M** a year.

Example 2: **Responded to 35,000+ customer inquiries** a year with **95% closed** in one day.

Example 3: Plant **produced 35,000 tons** of liquid oxygen on average over last five years.

Example 4: **Launched two new FDA approved drugs** that garnered **$5M** in new annual revenues and **4%** new market share.

Did you notice that each example always begins with an action verb. Never begin an accomplishment with I led, I did, I completed. We already know it's you.

Below is what you **DO NOT** want an accomplishment to look like:

**I led a major customer project that was a success and it had a positive impact on all departments to include their purchasing, legal, finance and administration team. It was a key strategic win for our firm.**

Here's my criticism: Eliminate the word I. **NEVER** use **success** on a resume. Everything on your resume better be a success. You could insert success in every single accomplishment. What does **positive** mean? Was money saved and if so how much? If it impacted all departments, why are you now listing them all? Try to keep your accomplishment to two sentences or less.

Now, look at a much better way from the above example to write this accomplishment:

**Led a strategic project for a $5M client and achieved a 15% reduction in cost savings the first year across all functions.**

Here's another version just reordered differently:

**Achieved a 15% cost savings by leading a strategic project for a $5M client impacting all of their functions.**

This time we are very tight on leading with an action, eliminating the need for the second sentence, providing scope about the client, quantifying the cost savings and summarizing the impact area. The second version of the accomplishment places more emphasis on ensuring the quantification comes early in the sentence.

Let's now review an example of what a final list of five Key Accomplishments should look like:

Ed Samuel

## Key Accomplishments

- Initiated a cost reduction program for a $10B telecommunications firm that saved $50M in the first 18 months
- Reduced client returns by 45% by shifting to two (2) new sourcing vendors
- Led implementation of SAP's demand planning $1M project and completed it on time and within budget
- Saved seven (7) lives by administering CPR at a regional drug treatment center over a 15-year period
- Closed $1B+ in surgical medical device sales with three (3) global firms

The last accomplishment listed is worthy to be discussed further. In this case, a medical sales leader worked at three separate firms for over twenty years. You are allowed to add up the sales from each of those firms and then show it as one number on this part of the resume as a Key Accomplishment. What you must do is ensure that if you add up the number at the three firms on your resume, the total then amounts to the large number you stated as a key accomplishment. Likewise, **ALL** of your Key Accomplishments need to be mapped back to the job and firm to those places on the resume.

---

## Principles – Key Accomplishments and Value Proposition

1. Focus on what you did and its quantified results.

2. Remember, an accomplishment without quantification is an activity with no value.

3. Always put accomplishments in priority and impact order—your biggest and then the second biggest, then third.

4. If in doubt, guestimate and use sound logic.

5. Be conservative when it comes to numbers or percentages.

6. Never use words like success or successful as everything needs to be viewed as successful, not just selected accomplishments.

7. Make sure each Key Accomplishment can be mapped back to the job and firm somewhere else on your resume as the first accomplishment listed.

8. Never go to three sentences for an accomplishment and get into a level of detail that should be saved for an interview.

9. Make a concerted effort to have white space on 50% of your accomplishments by keeping to one to two sentences whenever possible.

10. An accomplishment is always written in past tense, even if you are working currently.

11. Never MIX your accomplishments and responsibilities.

12. Avoid using these words: many, few, all and some. When you have the opportunity, always be definitive and quantify how many with a number.

# Optimizing Your Resume

# Chapter 7
## Firm or Organization and Employment Timeframes

*"It is better to fail in originality than to succeed in imitation."*
Herman Melville

You first need to declare the current or last firm or organization you worked at and the total years of employment. The name should be easy to look up on the internet and not a fictitious one. State the location of where you worked. Then provide a brief one-line summary of the type of company or organization. Below is an example of what it should look like:

**Gibson Supply, West Grove, PA            2000 - 2019**
Regional building supply wholesale distributor with 10 locations.

Providing a brief description and scope of the concern tells the reader some initial context for the breadth, size and scope of the organization. If the firm is public, you can also state revenue and/or number of employees. For private firms, you would leave these off unless financial information has been made public in some form.

Here is one more example of a publicly traded firm:

**Johnson Computer Services, Wyalusing, PA   1998 - 2019**
IT services security firm with $250M in revenues serving eastern USA.

    I always prefer you declare the town and state where you physically worked the majority of the time. Avoid entering the city and state of where the headquarters is located. The reason is that it may throw the person off if you say you are from Greater Cleveland, Ohio and your last job says you worked at Tampa, FL. Don't create a question mark as to where you literally live today. As you are starting to realize, I am not a fan of creating confusion or questions and having a hiring manager or recruiter try to figure things out since it leads to frustration and is never positive.

    As to years of service, I am a stickler for being TRUTHFUL on a resume in all ways, especially how long you worked somewhere. This may sound straightforward but there is a circle of career coaches that will tell you to "only show 15 years on a resume." What happens next is cringe worthy.

    Here's a real-life example. A person started work for a large global firm in 1985 and was laid off in 2018. On this resume, they only show 2003 – 2018. The reader thought they only worked there fifteen years. This is a smoke and mirror tactic that almost always ends up as a non-starter once the firm, hiring manger or recruiter figures it all out. I usually hear the reason used is that the work a person has done prior to the fifteen years ago is not relevant to the job he or she is moving forward into. I could not DISAGREE more on this line of thinking. Most of the time, everything you have done has relevance when you're doing a good job articulating your value proposition.

I will be addressing how Early Career should be handled later in this book but for now, please be truthful as to the length you worked at any firm, no matter how far back it goes.

---

## Principles – Firm or Organization and Employment Timeframes

1. **Add a company name that can be found by searching the internet unless you were self-employed without a website.**

2. **Insert the city and state where you physically worked, not the corporate location (unless you worked there).**

3. **Always put actual years worked at a firm—start to finish—even if it was more than fifteen years.**

4. **Insert a brief summary of the firm or organization and add breadth and scope whenever possible.**

# Chapter 8
# Job Titles, Responsibilities and Accomplishments

*"Do you have a smoke detector for your career?"*
Ed Samuel

It's important that you insert a title on your resume for your current job or your last job and the years you were in that role. The title should be stated such that if a new employer was to conduct a background check, then it should align with the job title the company used for you. There are firms that have harsh background checks and if you were to misstate your title and/or the years you were in that role on your resume and it was confirmed as inaccurate, it could result in the nixing of any potential job offer.

Here's an example of how it should look. Let's assume this person was at the firm for ten years but was only a manager the last five years.

**Controller** (2014-Present)

There are firms or organizations that have unique job titling as a result of their culture or practices. Typically, when this occurs the internal job titles do not align well with the job titles in the broader marketplace. As an example, there are firms that call every leader a team leader. They do not use supervisor, manager, vice president—ever. But at most other firms that same team leader would hold a far different and higher-level title. You do have a right to call yourself what the market should know you for based on the work that you conduct or have conducted. In these situations, you are allowed to state the correct job title on your resume BUT you must also recognize the firm's official title given to you. Here is an example of what to do in this case.

**Controller – Team Leader** (2014-Present)

If the work you did was truly Controller duties as defined by the marketplace, call yourself a Controller but insert with a dash or parenthesis the title that the firm officially uses.

The next step is to focus in on the gross responsibilities in the role in a concise way. Even though assumptions can be drawn based on a title, there are nuances that can be significant when explaining the breadth, scope and duties assigned in that position. For most positions, there is a formal job description. Your goal is to take that job description and summarize it in five lines with the most important details. Let's look at an example below.

**Controller**
Managed accounting that included profit and loss reporting, account reconciliations, monthly closes, accounts payable, internal controls, interfacing with external auditors and cash flow analysis. Led team of six; two senior accountants, A/P Manager and three accounting clerks. Member of corporate governance committee.

It's important that you call out the work that literally consumed most of your time and don't accentuate the minor work that you did. If you led a team, always highlight how many people you led and call out the key players on your team by title. If you are on a key internal committee, specify it.

If you are working in your job currently, then state everything in present tense. If you are no longer at a firm or in the job state everything in past tense. Do not mix past and present in the responsibility section.

When a role is supporting a specific division, department or location, it's key that you call it out as part of your job title. When you don't call it out, then it's assumed you were in this role supporting the entire company. But, if in reality, it was only a part of the company, it misleads people that you played a larger role when that was not the case. Here is an example of what it should look like if supporting a division or part of the firm.

**Controller (Automotive Division)**
Managed accounting that included profit and loss reporting, account reconciliations, monthly closes, accounts payable, internal controls, interfacing with external auditors and cash flow analysis. Led team of six; two senior accountants, A/P Manager and three accounting clerks. Member of Corporate Governance Committee.

Let's use a different example of where you can call out other details about the breadth and scope. This time we will focus on a person who is currently a Supply Chain Manager as part of a larger US wide firm.

**Supply Chain Manager**
Lead all aspects of supply chain strategy across 10 manufacturing plants, 1000 product skews and 250 vendors. Champion process efficiencies and cost reduction initiatives using Six Sigma. Collaborate with customer service, materials

and purchasing. Manage a budget of $1M annually. Member of SAP and raw material committee.

Another common mistake is to use words that are not necessary. For example, severely limit the use of the word "the." You will be amazed at how much white space you free when eliminating "the." Once more, do not use the infamous no-no word, "successful" or "successfully" for reasons stated in the previous chapter.

Also, whenever possible **refrain from using ALL CAPS** constantly. All caps can be a major distraction to the reader since more often than not, readers will be looking only at the words in ALL CAPS and not reading the entire section. A common mistake made on resumes is to put every key word in Capital letters. I recommend just the opposite even if technically it's a proper name simply because it distracts the reader to see only those key words. We want the reader to read all of it, not part of it.

Let's look at what **not to do**. The **mistakes** made are highlighted in **bold**.

**Supply Chain Manager**
I lead all aspects of **the** supply chain strategy **for my firm** across 10 manufacturing plants, 1000 product skews and 250 vendors. **I** champion process efficiencies and cost reduction initiatives using Six Sigma. **Successfully** collaborate with customer service, materials and purchasing. Manage a budget of $1M annually. Member of **the** SAP and **R**aw **M**aterial **C**ommittee.

It's imperative you remove as many unneeded words as possible. You want it to be tight and not long. These extra words act as fillers and do not add real value.

There is one more very common mistake made when responsibilities are mixed in with accomplishments. Here's an example of what not to do. The accomplishments are bolded.

**Supply Chain Manager**
Led all aspects of supply chain strategy across 10 manufacturing plants and 1000 product skews. **Implemented SAP materials module with a team of 10 people.** Championed process efficiencies **and reduced costs by $10M in first 3 years.** Collaborated with customer service, materials and purchasing. **Consistently came under budget** of $1M annually. Member of SAP and raw material committee.

The far better way of expressing responsibilities and accomplishments is to simply keep them separated. Let's look at the same example stated correctly as follows:

**Supply Chain Manager**
Lead all aspects of supply chain strategy across 10 manufacturing plants, 1000 product skews and 250 vendors. Champion process efficiencies and cost reduction initiatives using Six Sigma. Collaborate with customer service, materials and purchasing. Manage a budget of $1M annually. Member of SAP and raw material committee.

- Implemented SAP materials module with a team of 10 people.
- Led two (2) initiatives that reduced costs by $10M in first 3 years.
- Came under budget by less than 1% consistently over 5-year period.

Once you have written the key responsibilities for a role in those five tight lines, you are ready to call out your most impactful accomplishments.

## Optimizing Your Resume

**GO BACK to Chapter 6** and use the identical approach and principles to construct all key accomplishments for each job that you have held. The key is to ask yourself this question for each job: "While I was in this job, what are the greatest accomplishments that had the most profound impact in a quantifiable way to the firm, division, group or organization that I supported?"

These accomplishments should also be in rank order with the most impactful one listed first taken right from your **Top 5 Accomplishments** list if applicable for that job. Never list accomplishments under a job randomly. The best is first, then the second best, third best, and so on.

Here is a rule of thumb when trying to determine how many accomplishments should be listed for each job you have held:

| Time with firm | # of Accomplishments |
|---|---|
| < 1 year | 1-2 |
| 1 year | 1-3 |
| 5 years | 4-5 |
| 10 years | 8-9 |
| 15 years | 12 |
| 20 years | 16 |
| 25 years | 20 |

A common mistake is to list too many accomplishments for being in a job a year or less. I've seen people list ten accomplishments in their most recent job that they held for only six months at the expense of the more impactful accomplishments from their previous job getting pushed to page two of the resume. For most hiring managers, they do not expect you to have accomplished miracles in such a short time.

## Principles – Job Titles, Responsibilities and Accomplishments

1. Always state the exact job title and years that you worked in the role to ensure there is never an issue when a background check is performed.

2. Never mix accomplishments with responsibilities.

3. Always state a job title that aligns to the work you did in the marketplace regardless of the title the firm or organization used – but still acknowledge the official company title.

4. Keep the job responsibilities to a tight five lines and call out breadth and scope whenever possible.

5. Avoid any and all unnecessary words like "the", "I", "our or my firm" and never use the word "successfully".

6. Use good judgment by not overstating the number of accomplishments based on the length of time you worked at a firm or organization.

7. Only identify and list the very best accomplishments in rank order in the role that you played – never in random order.

# Optimizing Your Resume

# Chapter 9
# Early Career

*"In youth we learn; in age we understand."*
Marie von Ebner-Eschenbach

For those who have work experience that is greater than twenty years, it poses a question, "How much of my prior and early career experience should be listed on the resume?" I contend the right answer will always be "it depends."

I've said earlier, I do not fall into the camp of those who believe you should only put the last fifteen years of experience on a resume. It simply is a flat-out mistake and creates all kinds of challenges for you as the candidate and the decision maker. I also believe it calls out an immediate integrity concern or a question of, "what are you hiding?" Any time an initial impression is made on a resume, I want it to be a positive one and not negative.

I understand there are two lines of thinking about only showing the last fifteen years on a resume. One has to do with the age bias concern. The other has to do with the notion that what you did sixteen years ago has little to no bearing on the new opportunity for which you are now searching.

# Optimizing Your Resume

I agree there is an age bias when searching for a job and people are gun shy in declaring how many years of experience they have. Let's say you trick the decision maker and you get the phone screen or face to face interview. Then, you are asked the question, "Where did you go to work after college?" Next thing you know, you are now declaring everything you should have stated on your resume the first time. If the decision makers have an age bias, do you think it goes away then? It does not and they will find a convenient reason for not selecting you and moving you forward. You will then get the infamous reply, "Sorry, but we have found more qualified candidates." You have thus wasted valuable job search time going down a path that would have been avoided if you had declared the truth on your resume.

As to the second rationale of not sharing the depth of your experience prior to sixteen years ago, it is also flat out wrong. In fact, I would contend just the opposite. Most decision makers are very curious and want to know your "full" story and not just one-third of it taken out of context. Another reason is that the job you held 30-25-20 years ago could be absolutely relevant to the work you are aiming to do next. An example would be if you were an engineer and spent your formative years at GE for the first ten years and then moved to the next firm for the last fifteen years. It would make no sense at all to not tell the reader of the resume that you worked for one of the greatest innovative engineering firms in the world. In this case I'd even explain responsibilities and specific accomplishments.

If you need to set a rule, then **ALWAYS go back twenty years** in listing your detailed experience in terms of responsibilities and accomplishments. Then, prior to that use good judgment to further call out your experience in detail as explained in the above GE example. But, please stay away from an across the board notion that you only show fifteen years on a resume.

Once you do land on how many years you want to declare in detail for each job and firm, there may yet be even earlier career experiences you want to capture, just not at that same level of detail. I want to offer a way to express **EARLY CAREER** on a resume in two forms that allow you to consolidate parts of the resume and yet be truthful to the reader that you did hold positions at other firms without displaying all the details for each position.

Below is the first way to express early career on the resume:

## EARLY CAREER

**Accounting Lead,** Samuel CPA, Sugar Run, PA and **Accountant,** Troy Accounting Services, Towanda, PA.

In this example, you bold the job and insert the name and location of the firm or organization for which you worked. You don't have to declare the dates, but you are being honest that you held other jobs prior.

Below is a second way to express early career and be even more truthful about your age in the job market:

## EARLY CAREER

**Accounting Lead,** Samuel CPA, Sugar Run, PA (1985 – 1990) and **Accountant,** Troy Accounting Services, Towanda, PA (1990 – 1995).

In this case you are declaring the dates you worked at those firms.

Optimizing Your Resume

One last way to express early career using one of these two above methods is to also declare any noteworthy accomplishments in that time frame. But the caution here is to ONLY declare something very noteworthy so the decision maker knows that even in your formative years, you were having an impact. Below is an example:

### EARLY CAREER

**Accounting Lead,** Samuel CPA, Sugar Run, PA and
**Accountant,** Troy Accounting Services, Towanda, PA.

- Led project and implemented new General Ledger system.

---

## Principles – Early Career

1. **Never feel that you are forced to ONLY show fifteen years of experience in detail on your resume.**

2. **If you need to set a rule, show at least twenty years of detailed experience at all times. Use good judgment after that if more job and firm details make sense to display on the resume.**

3. **List both job title(s), firms and their locations.**

4. **Insert any substantial accomplishment(s) during the entire early career time period, but, only noteworthy ones.**

# Chapter 10
# **Education and Certifications**

*"An investment in knowledge pays the best interest."*
Ben Franklin

Listing your education and certification is straightforward at one level but there are nuances that you need to be aware of in both areas. Let's look at education first.

Below is an example of how I would want you to outline education on your resume:

### **EDUCATION**

Master of Science in Accountancy, Temple University, Philadelphia, PA
Bachelor of Science in Accounting, University of Wilmington, New Castle, DE
Associate in Accounting, Hessor College
Manchester, NH

There is really no need to use BA, BS, MSA if you are spelling it out. Always list your most current degree first, followed by next most recent to the last.

The question arises on whether to enter dates or not. If you have fifteen years or less of experience, go ahead and enter the dates; if more than fifteen years of experience, leave the dates off. Although I push for honesty all the time, there is no rule that says you have to put dates on the resume and in essence telegraph your exact age.

Another common mistake made on education is to omit the name of the degree. The reason this happens is because the person went to college and got a degree in Biology and now, twenty years later, he or she is the Director of Marketing and has made a career shift. Again, when you have nothing listed, it brings up the question, "What are you hiding?" and it's not positive. I'd rather have you declare what you got your degree in rather than leave it blank and let the decision maker know you made the career change and the reasons why during an interview.

In cases where there is no formal education after high school, then it's imperative that you indicate what high school you went to and if you have a diploma or GED. If you have listed any kind of formal education at a college or a university, then it's assumed you graduated from high school or hold a GED. Here is an example to use:

## EDUCATION

Diploma - Hillsborough High School, Hillsborough Township, NJ

The next area that comes up often are clients who have had some college or are currently attending college. It's important that you not confuse the reader and be clear as to your progress to date. Here's the first example:

## EDUCATION

Bachelor of Science in Accounting, University of Wilmington, New Castle, DE
- Currently enrolled, 80 credits completed, expected graduation, May 2020.

When it's stated this way, you are being very honest and telling the decision maker exactly what you have done and when you expect to complete your degree. Here is another example where a person took classes twenty years ago but never finished the degree:

## EDUCATION

Bachelor of Science in Accounting, University of Wilmington, New Castle, DE
- Completed 80 credits toward degree program

This way you are stating you were in a degree program and what you have completed. I've spoken to many people in this mode that are reluctant to state that they took "some college" classes because it calls out that they never finished. I hold the opposite view. By not listing it, the decision maker assumes you have done "nothing" to advance your educational skills at all, and I'd rather have something go up against nothing any time of the day on a resume. It conveys a much more positive image of you regardless of any and all issues that may have gotten in the way in finishing the degree.

Let's take a look at Certifications next. They are very important to list since some are required to perform certain jobs. In other cases, past certifications validate your commitment to the subject at that time of your career and your ability to pass the training.

Below is an example of how I would want you to outline certification on your resume:

### CERTIFICATIONS

Series 7, 63, 24 and 66 (active)
Certified Public Accountant (CPA), current license #123456, State of PA
Certified Management Accountant – CMA (inactive)

If you hold an active certification, I do recommend stating it. If you state any credential after your names at the top of your resume, it's "assumed" your certifications or licenses are active. Certain certifications like patent numbers are given to you and are public record. In those situations, declare your license number so a decision maker can google it and see that you are in fact, currently certified. Always be sure to double-check the internet yourself to make sure there is not a problem with a certification or license number being displayed.

If you held other certifications in the past and they are no longer active, please note it as inactive so as not to give an impression that it's active in any way. You want to list all active certifications first and then by dates obtained, then those that are inactive.

Similar to an educational degree in process, declare any certification in process. Here's an example:

### CERTIFICATIONS

Project Management Professional, PMI, NJ
- Core training completed; exam targeted for November 2019.

In cases where you have one college listed and one certification, you can collapse the two categories together on the resume as follows:

### EDUCATION and CERTIFICATIONS

Bachelor of Science in Accounting, University of Wilmington, New Castle, DE
Certified Public Accountant (CPA), current license #123456
State of PA

---

## Principles – Education and Certifications

1. Always declare the name of your degree.

2. **If you have taken college classes and not finished, still declare the credits obtained to date.**

3. **If you did not go to college, then declare that you have a diploma or GED.**

4. **Make sure you state if your certifications are active or inactive.**

5. **Declare your certification or license number and if it is a public record, check the internet to be sure you can validate it.**

# Optimizing Your Resume

## Chapter 11
## **Awards**

*"People work for money but go the extra mile for recognition, praise and rewards."*
Dale Carnegie

Awards can be a tricky area for many when it comes to your resume. I've had cases where clients have not called out awards at all that they won or earned. I have had other cases where awards are mixed into responsibilities and accomplishments and literally lost in the detail. I also had just the opposite, when someone will list every single award and it literally takes up the entire page of a resume.

**I define an award this way**: Any public recognition internally or externally where you were asked to come up front in a room, meeting or convention and handed a plaque or letter of recognition or received one in writing from the President, CEO, Board or Executive Leadership team or a public forum or organization.

Let's deal with each of the above problems one by one.

The first problem is when no awards are declared on the resume at all. I'll ask the question, "It seems odd to me that

Optimizing Your Resume

with all of your accomplishments at these noteworthy firms, you have never received an award?" Then if I probe a bit harder, I'll get back, "Well, I did win the President's award at GE back in 1990, but that's too old to bring up." I could **NOT disagree** more. Earning an award means that at that time, you rose up to a higher level than your peers and did "something of tangible merit" which is part of your success story and value proposition. The other issue I will hear is, "I don't want to brag." Again, I could **NOT disagree more**. You should never feel embarrassed to think you are showboating or bragging if what you did is true and factual.

The second problem deals with mixing in awards with accomplishments or declaring the award itself as an accomplishment. Let's look at an example of what not to do:

**Shell and Smith Company**

- Won salesperson of the year in 2018.

I do endorse this as a tangible accomplishment that will impress the decision maker, but it does not add to your value proposition at all. The winning of the award may be a personal accomplishment but at face value it has no value. What you want to do on a resume is to declare what you specifically did to earn the award—therein lies the real value. Here it is restated as part of an accomplishment:

**Shell and Smith Company**

- Exceeded stretch goal of $1M in new account sales, 2018 (#1 out of 52 sales reps).

Later on in the resume after **Education and Certifications**, you can then add the following:

## AWARDS

- Employee of the Year, 2012, Shell and Smith Company

The last problem with awards is when there are simply too many, you have to streamline them. The best way to do this is to consolidate them. Put them in logical groupings and state the total number of awards won at that firm. Here's an example of what to do:

## AWARDS

- Employee of the Year, 2012, Shell and Smith Company
- **Five** Spot Awards for Excellence, 2000-2012, Society for College Financial Management

Finally, there are situations in which you have literally won dozens of awards, especially when in a sales-oriented capacity, when you will need to call out the five biggest ones and then add the word "Selected." This can hold true in other parts of the resume as well. Here is an example of what it would look like:

## AWARDS - Selected

- Employee of the Year, 2012, Shell and Smith Company
- Five (5) Spot Awards for Excellence, 2000-2012, Society for Financial Management
- Ace Award for best invention, 2000, GE
- Pace Employee Award for highest sales growth, 1999, GE
- Outstanding Community Volunteer, 1999, Los Angeles Chamber of Commerce

## Principles – Awards

1. Declare any public award earned no matter how far back.
2. Consolidate multiple awards whenever possible.

3. Always declare the company or organization where you won the award.

4. Cap your awards to a total of five and if more add - Selected.

# Chapter 12
# Professional Development

*"In this world you're either growing or you're dying, so get in motion and grow. "*
Lou Holtz

In the course of a person's work life, many people are given or seize the opportunity to continue to sharpen their "saws" on technical or leadership competencies. In certain cases, the classes may be mandated from a compliance standpoint. In other cases, the Board of Directors may recommend that once executives achieve a certain level, they must attend a nationally recognized executive leadership program if they want to continue to advance.

When I see professional development missing on a resume, I am concerned that a hiring manager may think that you literally have done "nothing" after college to sharpen your saw in any form. Now, in all fairness sometimes that is the case, but most of the time, my clients will tell me they did do some development work over the years. I love it when we have this discussion since we are pulling out more depth in a person's value. Unfortunately, when I ask clients, "Why are you not declaring this important part on your resume?" I will get an answer back that someone told me the resume "had to be two pages in length." Brevity is not a good reason to mask this part of you.

What I use as a rule to constitute professional development on a resume is a class that is no less than four hours long or ideally one that is one to three days to a week or more in length. Many executive leadership programs can last up to five consecutive weeks. You want to exclude one-hour long webinars or workshops and really hone in on some meaningful development.

Let's look at an example of what this section of the resume should look like:

### PROFESSIONAL DEVELOPMENT

- Conflict Management, Smith Conflict Learning Center, MA
- Managing Personal Growth, Blessing and Smith, NJ
- Advanced Leadership and Decision Making, General Electric, PA
- High Performance Teams, Blessing and Smith, NJ

It's always good to declare who led the training whether it be an outside learning organization or an internal training within your firm. In cases where you simply can't remember but you know you took the training and it was a while ago, I'd rather have you list it and talk to it if asked than exclude it. Like with Awards and many other sections of your resume, limit a long list to no more than five areas in which you obtained training over the years. Try to focus on the ones that had the most impact on you.

## Principles – Professional Development

1. Never omit key developments on your resume for the reason of keeping your resume to only two pages. Remember "nothing" never equals "something."

2. Focus on up to five developmental learning classes or seminars that were most important to your growth—ideally classes that were a half-day, full day, week or more in length.

3. If at all possible, identify not only the topic area but who delivered the training.

# Optimizing Your Resume

# Chapter 13
## **Technical Skills**

*"It is true that the mental aspect of kung-fu is the desired end;
however, to achieve this end, technical skill must come first."*
Bruce Lee

There are certain positions that require a level of technical skill that you need to declare on a resume since many times they are required for you to even be considered a candidate. In other cases, you may have had technical training and knowledge in the past that you still want people to know about. Traditionally IT oriented roles can be quite detailed, followed by roles in compliance to roles that on the surface require little or no technical skills. The majority of the time, many technical skills fall in software-oriented applications. There are exceptions such as a scientist who is trained on certain types of microscopes or a metallurgist who is trained on a certain type of forging press.

I encourage clients to call out technical skills in which they have a working knowledge—especially if that skill is required in the job. I don't encourage listing any technical skills that have "topical or surface level knowledge" or something you have had no practical experience using. Let's look at an example as follows:

Optimizing Your Resume

## TECHNICAL SKILLS

Advanced Excel, Oracle Financials, ACT, Saleforce.com, Hyperion, PowerCampus

In this case, the candidate is calling out a variety of software tools he has used in the past, two of which are CRM tools, another that supports the educational industry and one that is used universally. If you are pursuing a job and it requires use of a CRM oriented tool as well, you are giving the decision maker some assurances that you are versed in either the same software tool or you have knowledge of how a similar tool is used.

Another common issue that surfaces is many software tools are home grown at a firm and are not known in the marketplace. In those cases, still list the name of the internal software tool and then in parenthesis the skill to which it relates. Here's an example:

## TECHNICAL SKILLS

Advanced Excel, Jonah (CRM), Champion (ERP), Voltage (Data Analytics)

In this next example below, the skill pertains much more to someone who has depth in information technology (IT) related software systems.

## TECHNICAL SKILLS

Oracle/JD Edwards ERP, SAP ERP, Siemens/Camstar MES, Wonderware Control Systems, IBM Connections, Visio, MS Project, MindManager, Software AG ARIS Business, MS SQL Server, Oracle Discoverer, DataStream, Taleo, AON Benefits, HR Case Management, Salesforce, Anaqua, Upside and HP-UX

As a rule, I always want to see the technical skills displayed on the second or third page of a resume for this chief reason—a technical skill displayed is not so different than an award. By itself it has no inherent value proposition. It's what you have done using it that becomes your accomplishment and where the true value is found. The other reason is that when technical skills are front and center on page one of your resume, it can drive home a thought the leadership, teaming and softer skills are a distance second. In many firms, the teaming traits needed trump the technical knowledge in importance.

## Principles – Technical Skills

1. **Only list those skills that you have hands-on knowledge and experience using.**

2. **Avoid putting all your technical skills and the entire category on Page 1 of your resume.**

3. **Validate the precise and proper name of any software or skill listed on the Internet unless it is a home-grown internal software or technical product.**

# Optimizing Your Resume

# Chapter 14
# **Presentations and Publications**

*"Get it down. Take chances. It may be bad, but it's the only way you can do anything really good. "*
William Faulkner

An opportunity to showcase your industry knowledge and depth of experience is to identify any public presentations and written publications you have done outside of the firms or organizations you have worked.

Let's focus on Presentations first. These are situations where you have been asked to go to a forum on a regional, national or global stage and present to an audience of your peers in the industry. Again, these are not internal presentations inside an organization where you have worked. The reason these presentations are so important is that your peers in the industry are now viewing you as a thought leader. This then says that you are not viewed as only special at the firm where you work or used to work but by the very competition that you go up against, support or collaborate with in some fashion.

The other consideration under this category is that you can broaden it by capturing all forms of communication when you spoke as an industry leader. For example, you may have given an interview on local and/or regional TV, cable or radio. These are other great ways to let the decision maker know you are putting yourself out there as a leader in your field.

Here's an example of how it should look on your resume:

## PRESENTATIONS

Shaping Employee Retention for Millenniums, Global SHRM Conference, July 2017
Ethics in the Workplace, National Human Resources Conference, Sept 2015
Interview on CNBN Cable News, Topic: Diversity and Hiring, June 2014.

It's important that you declare the name of your presentation or topic, the name of the organization sponsoring and running the event and the date and year you spoke. Many times, the internet will retain conference information, TV, cable and radio broadcasts. You want to be as accurate as possible in case the reader was to search on the internet. The more detail you show, the more credence you get by the reader of the resume.

Like with the other categories mentioned earlier, if you spoke at far more than five events, select the best of the best for the resume and then add the word – Selected.

Even if you only spoke at five events in total, there is no hard and fast rule that says you must list all of them. You can list one or two or whatever. The key is to list the ones that have earned you the greatest industry buzz or recognition.

Let's shift to publications. These are examples of something that you officially published outside of your firm or organization on a regional, national or global level within your industry. Examples of publications include magazines, local or national newspapers, technical journals, white papers or even an online blog post.

I recommend that you note the title of the article, name of publication, month and year of publication, page number and include a URL if it is accessible via the internet.

Here's an example of how it should look on your resume:

## PUBLICATIONS

Impact of Coal on the Environment, *Coal Monthly*, Sept. 2013, pp. 56-66.
The New Era of Coal Extraction, *Scranton Tribune-Times*, Aug. 2010, pp. 1, 4.

Like with presentations, the more detail you can share to validate the authenticity of the publication, the better. In addition, if you wrote down more than five publications, pick the ones that have the greatest impact, reach and depth of your industry expertise, then add the word – Selected.

---

## Principles – Presentations and Publications

1. **Select those that have the best depiction of your industry depth and expertise.**

2. **Provide as much detail as possible to show authenticity and validation via the internet whenever possible.**

# Optimizing Your Resume

# Chapter 15
# **Patents**

*"There are no rules. That is how art is born, how breakthroughs happen. Go against the rules or ignore the rules. That is what invention is about."*
Helen Frankenthaler

In cases where you hold a patent, it's imperative that you declare them on your resume. Patents are common with engineers, designers, scientists and those in research and development across almost all industries. The reason you state them on your resume is that it demonstrates your deep industry expertise and your ability to create a competitive advantage.

One mistake I've seen with patents is that sometimes they are listed on one's resume with little to no mention of the business impact under the accomplishment section. An example: I had a client, a scientist, note a patent on his resume. When I asked him about the impact of the patent, he finally said it generated half of the firm's revenue for ten years and reaped 75% of the market share. Somehow, none of this was stated as an accomplishment on his resume up until that point. In other cases, I've asked the question, and from a pure research and development standpoint it can be very hard to discern the impact. So, it's not one size fits all as much as thoughtful dialogue that can help develop the impact of a patent.

Here is an example of what a patent should look like on your resume:

### PATENTS - SELECTED

Corrugated Vent Method (#9,099, 999), Section Vent (#9,098,098)

The number (#) listed **MUST BE** found in the US Patent database at: http://patft.uspto.gov.

One other problem that I've seen over the years is that when a patent is listed, like in the above example, it is assumed that you personally were responsible for it. However, if more than one person was involved, then you need to declare it as a team patent. Below is how I recommend that it be listed in this case:

### PATENTS – SELECTED

Corrugated Vent Semi-Method, Team, (#9,099, 991), Section Vent, (#9,098,098)

---

# Principles – Patents

1. **Whenever possible, declare the results of the patent in the accomplishment sections of your resume.**
2. **Always state if your patent was a team effort or not.**

3. **Be sure to validate the patent number on <u>http://patft.uspto.gov</u>**

# Optimizing Your Resume

# Chapter 16
# Professional Organizations

*"...throughout my career, it felt like I did my best to align myself with quality artists, quality work, and it is a situation of steel sharpening steel.*
Unknown

As you go throughout your career, you will be given the opportunity to join professional organizations that are aligned to your industry. In addition, you may also be a member of cross-industry organizations or forums that continue to grow and strengthen your skills and competencies. Being part of these organizations also reinforces any statements you make about being on the leading edge of your industry.

If you don't belong to any kind of organization where you are rubbing elbows with the competition, then it's a harder argument to make to a potential hiring manager about your industry depth. The other caution is that if you work at a mid-size to large firm and spend 100% of your time ONLY accumulating knowledge internally and never stepping out, then you can be viewed as insulated to a great degree. For some hiring managers, that type of insulation is not viewed favorably.

I prefer that you list industry-oriented organizations first followed by non-industry ones. I also want you to include any leadership roles that you held within these organizations.

Here's an example of how professional organizations should be shown on your resume:

## PROFESSIONAL ORGANIZATIONS

SEC Compliance Association, Philadelphia Chapter, Vice President of Membership, 2017
Pennsylvania Institute of Certified Public Accountants
Toastmasters Club, Baltimore East, MD, former President, 2015-2016

I also want you to list organizations on which you have once served but of which you may no longer be a part. The reason why is it tells a decision maker that although no longer active, you have taken a portion of your career to rub shoulders with other industry experts at some point in time.

I recently worked with a client who was a member of an industry focused professional organization for the last fifteen years. Her firm paid for the yearly membership of $1000. When she was down-sized she could no longer be an active member of this organization and did not want to show it on her resume. We ended up fixing and adding it to her resume and made a note that she was active from 2000-2015.

Again, keep in mind that when you present "nothing" on a resume, it will never mean "something" to a reader.

## Principles – Professional Organizations

1. Be part of at least one industry-focused professional organization to demonstrate to a potential employer how you keep your saw sharpened.

2. Declare any leadership role that you hold currently or have held in the past.

3. Show organizations in which you were active even if you're not active currently.

4. Always list industry organizations first followed by non-industry ones.

# Optimizing Your Resume

## Chapter 17
## Volunteer and Community

*"Life's most persistent and urgent question is, "What are you doing for others?"*
Martin Luther King, Jr.

One of the most important parts of a resume is the very end when you list work that you have done as a volunteer to help those in need, your community, the environment, your church, mosque, synagogue or temple and even, believe it or not, your political party.

I have seen hundreds of resumes where this area is not addressed, yet I believe it's a **BIG mistake**. I even devoted an entire segment on my Philadelphia radio program to the need to include volunteer work on your resume.

There are three overarching reasons I believe you need to do it. The first pertains to how you treat other human beings and/or the environment. Do you have a heart, and do you do anything other than focus on work and more work outside of your family on your personal time? A thoughtful hiring manager can make a connection that if you make time to help and treat people with kindness, you just might bring that same heart in to the organization or the team you lead or serve.

The second reason is that when you volunteer, you may be doing far more than a certain kind of task. You might be leading a project or have some formal leadership role at the church. This also gives an impression to a potential hiring manager about other skills and abilities you have outside of the expected job function that serve in the workplace.

The third reason is much more pragmatic. It's not legal in most states but it happens all the time. Let's say it comes down to you and another for a job. Everything matches up in terms of accomplishments, value proposition, personality and fit, technical competencies and education and there is an impasse. Finally, the hiring manager's boss comes into the room and plays the role of tie breaker. She looks at one resume and then the other and says hire this one. Everyone asks why. She says, "because they volunteer for this cause and the other person does not volunteer at all." Afterwards, the candidate who was hired jumped onto that boss's public profile and sure enough, she happened to support the same cause. Do not underestimate that certain leaders support causes and have a heart; show them that you do the same.

Unfortunately, when I ask people about why they did not add their volunteer work, I get the infamous, "Well I was told my resume had to be two pages and thus we had no room." This is simply crazy. I've personally seen volunteer work listed on a resume foster more conversation during and after an interview and be the final "unofficial" reason why someone was selected to get the job offer. Sadly, when I push clients in this area, it's amazing the good work they do that up until that moment would not have been listed on their resume.

Let's look at an example of what should be on the resume:

Ed Samuel

## **VOLUNTEER and COMMUNITY**

Breakfast Mission, Wilmington, DE
Autism Foundation, Philadelphia, PA, annual fund raiser leader
Bible Church of Wyalusing, Sugar Run, PA, mission trip leader – led seven trips

Again, like in other areas of the resume, you never want to show more than five areas you are supporting, and if more than five, add the word – Selected. The only exception would be certain roles that require and expect you to be connected to a large list of community-based support organizations. Ideally, I prefer that you show only three areas in this section to not overstate the effort that you do outside of work and family time which may lend an impression that it might bleed into work hours in some way.

Every once in a while, I will work with someone who focuses on work and family and their only volunteer efforts are for a political party. Even then, I would err on listing it rather than not. I understand the bias argument but stating you are involved in something is better than not being involved in anything. The only exception would be alignment or declaration to an organization that is generally viewed as highly divisive by the populace. My overall thought: remember if you have listed "nothing" it will never resonate into "something."

Lastly, for those who do literally nothing outside of work and family, I beg you to do something with an organization in the community. You do not have to make it an all or nothing arrangement. Spend one hour every three months at the local food bank or breakfast mission to help. Once you do so, you get to put it down. If you want to spend more time, that's even better. I have never met anyone who did not go down this path that did not come out on the other side a better human being, teammate or leader.

---

## Principles – Volunteer and Community

1. **Never leave this section blank on a resume, especially if the reasoning is your resume must only be two pages.**

2. **If you do nothing at all outside of work or family today, please find one organization and do something for it weekly, monthly, quarterly or even annually.**

3. **Don't be afraid to list who you help even if it's for your church, temple, synagogue or mosque.**

4. **Try to limit your list to three organizations so it does not seem overwhelming.**

Ed Samuel

# Chapter 18
## Standards: Look, Feel and Length

*"Be a yardstick of quality. Some people aren't used to an environment where excellence is expected."*
Steve Jobs

I am a stickler with keeping to a consistent look and feel for each page of a resume and holding to all standards from top to bottom—everything from spacing and spelling to alignment and consistency. You don't want the reader to be distracted with inconsistencies, readability or quality concerns—especially if the average time to screen a resume is seven seconds.

I was in Arizona a few years ago and was asked to review a resume for a friend. He had applied for a regional role at a large box chain. After my review, I spoke to him on the phone and suggested he make some immediate changes. One of these was that he had spelled the name of his previous company wrong in a couple of places. He called me a few days later, telling me he had already turned it in before I corrected it. He said, "I wished I had spoken to you earlier. The box store told me that they would not be moving me forward. They saw inconsistencies and spelling errors on the resume, and it was simply unacceptable." The irony is that this person was a true

## Optimizing Your Resume

leader and had done some amazing work, but he treated the resume poorly and did not invest the amount of time needed to make it an excellent example of his work with high standards and a high-quality look and feel.

Here is a list of standards and guidelines to use to ensure your resume is of the highest quality:

1. Use consistent Font Sizes. I prefer Cambria 11 for the bulk of the resume, Cambria 12 for Category headings, Cambria 10 for Firm or Organization descriptors, Cambria 18 for your Job Title and Cambria 22 for your Name.

2. Keep spacing consistent throughout the entire document and each section.

3. Be consistent in quantification. Example: $1K $10K $100K $1M $50M

4. When calling out a number from 1-9, say one (1), two (2). Once you hit 10, then just state the number.

5. Avoid creating a dense resume with each accomplishment filling up two full lines. Try to alternate one-line accomplishments with a one-and-a-half line accomplishments to create white space and more balance.

6. Only **BOLD** your Name, Titles and Categories Headings.

7. Limit the use of ALL CAPS and Capital Letters if at all possible.

8. Always add a Header to the second and third page of a resume with your name on the left and your email address on the right.

9. Add pages numbers on pages 2 and 3 at bottom right.

10. Always provide a ½ inch of white space at the bottom of a resume. Let words bleed over to next page so that there is no appearance of text being smushed.

11. No spelling or grammar errors – no exceptions

12. Have at least one professional or third-party use this list to edit your resume.

13. Have two resumes: one to share and send to firms, the other a plain text resume used for uploading into applicant tracking systems.

---

## Principles – Standards: Look, Feel and Length

1. **Adhere to all 13 standards listed above—no exceptions.**

2. **Have an administrative expert review your resume as a double-check and new set of eyes to ensure standards are being followed.**

# Optimizing Your Resume

# Chapter 19
# Resume Sections and Template

*"Organizing is what you do before you do something, so that when you do it, it is not all mixed up."*
A. A. Milne

Your resume is broken into many sections. Some sections are mandatory and others are optional depending on your situation.

Below is the complete list:

**Name** – must have

**Title** – must have

**Core Competencies** – must have

**Key Accomplishments** – must have

**Professional Experience** – must have

**Early Career** – optional if under 20 years, non-optional if greater than 20 years

**Education** – must have

**Certifications** – optional

**Awards** – optional

**Professional Development** – optional

**Technical skills** – must have (everyone needs to know Word and/or Excel)

**Presentations** – optional

**Publications** – optional

**Patents** – optional

**Professional Organizations** – optional

**Volunteer** – must have (even if you need to join one ASAP)

On the next page you will see an example of what a SamNova resume will look like when completed if you follow the principles and guidelines expressed in this book. This is only an example and not a real person. Everything stated has been included to provide you with an example of what your resume should look and feel like when completed. It also does not reflect all potential categories but a realistic sample of what a common resume can include.

492-910-0010

# Ed Samuel, CPA

Greater Denver, CO
linkedin.com/in/edsamuel/
esamuel@samnovainc.com

## COMPLIANCE DIRECTOR

Compliance and Operations leader with more than 19 years of experience supporting Fortune 500 financial services, investment and educational sectors. Expertise includes compliance, approving selected security transactions, leading internal regulations training, cyber-security, privacy, data protection, social media rules, external auditing coordination and conducting branch audits. Fluid in Spanish and French. Known for building strong relationships with advisors and keeping an enterprise in strong standing with the SEC.

## CORE COMPETENCIES

- Regulatory Compliance
- Financial Reporting
- Branch Audits
- Operational Compliance
- Data Protection
- Series 7, 63, 24 and 66
- Cyber-Security
- Quality Control
- Internal Audits

## KEY ACCOMPLISHMENTS

- Pivotal for ensuring merger of El Smith Investments and Samuel Securities involving 5,000 clients occurred seamlessly as part of $75M merger
- Conducted more than 30 audits at three (3) office locations with no material findings over last 5 years
- Led 24 compliance training classes, webinars and on-line conferences
- Improved compliance reviews by 75% within first 18-months
- Upgraded 115 operating systems and/or laptops to an advanced cyber-security protection program

## PROFESSIONAL EXPERIENCE

Samuel Securities, Denver, CO                                                2011 – Present
The 29th largest financial services firm in the Smith and Jones Securities Network, with $10B AUM.

**Director of Compliance** (2016 – Present)
Provide compliance support to more than 75 advisors serving 5,000 clients. Oversee compliance, approve selected security transactions, internal regulations training, cyber-security, privacy, data protection, social media rules, external auditing coordination and conduct branch audits with primary focus on securities, retirement, educational, and estate planning accounts for both individuals and business owners. Member of Smith and Jones audit committee and governance board.

- Pivotal for ensuring merger of El Smith Investments and Smith and Jones Securities involving 5,000 clients occurred seamlessly as part of $75M merger
- Conducted more than 30 audits at three (3) office locations with no material findings over last 5 years
- Led 24 compliance training classes, webinars and online conferences
- Improved compliance reviews by 75% within first 18-months
- Upgraded 115 operating systems and/or laptops to an advanced cyber-security protection program
- Improved Title IV compliance reviews by 75% with first 18 months
- Conducted more than 100 blotter reviews

**Senior Operations Specialist** (2011 – 2016)
As primary contact for ~5000 client accounts, audited and approved requests inclusive of portfolio allocations, reinstatements, stock and option trades and product information. Provided support to 50+ financial advisors. Provided audit and training support to compliance team. Served as focal point for computer equipment, security set up and application support for all new hires. Identified and initiated

# Optimizing Your Resume

**Ed Samuel**                                                                                    esamuel@samnovainc.com

process improvements to reduce cost and improve revenues. Member of IT audit committee.

- Reviewed and approved ~10,000 security oriented transactions annually
- Provided support to more than 150 audits
- Co-led and supported 25 major compliance training events
- Identified disability insurance issue that increased annual revenue by $100K
- Devised campaign to increase annual disability insurance revenue from ~200 house accounts

Society for College Financial Management, Pittsburgh, PA                          2000 – 2011
A $50M accounting services firm serving more than 50 colleges and universities.

**Accounting Manager** (2000 – 2011)
Provided oversight to all aspects of accounting to include; monthly closing, quarterly financial reporting, GAAP, client business analysis, bank reconciliations, accounts payable, accounts receivable, balance sheet and account reconciliations, establishing and monitoring internal controls and external audit coordination. Led team of seven (7) including an accounting supervisor and three (3) senior accountants. Member of corporate internal audit committee.

- Resolved a $1M bank reconciliation issue that had been unresolved for over 3-years
- Hired, trained and mentored six (6) accounting professionals
- Led initiative that reduced DSO from 90 days to less 40 over 18-month period
- Improved the month-end closing cycle by nine (9) days by implementing new accounting system
- Established 36 new internal control procedures and reduced risk reserves by $250K

Samuel College, Wyalusing, PA                                                                 1995 – 2000
A private college focused on information technology with 500 students.

**Accounting Supervisor** (1998 – 2000)
Oversaw monthly closing, account reconciliations, banking, accounts payable, petty cash, internal controls and balance sheet reporting. Led team of four (4) including two (2) accountants and two (2) accounts payable specialist. Member of internal controls committee.

- Reduced time to pay vendors by 45 days by creating an automated tickler system
- Met or exceeded monthly closing deadlines 30 consecutive months
- Resolved a $50K bank reconciliation error

**Senior Accountant** (1995 – 1998)
Responsible for processing journal entries, paying vendors and baseline balance sheet reporting.

- Resolved a $50K bank reconciliation error

## EARLY CAREER

**Accounting Lead,** Samuel CPA, Sugar Run, PA and **Accountant,** Troy Accounting Services, Towanda, PA.

## EDUCATION

Masters of Science in Accountancy, Temple University, Philadelphia, PA
Bachelors of Science in Accounting, University of Wilmington, New Castle, DE

## CERTIFICATIONS

Series 7, 63, 24 and 66 (active)
CPA License (#123456 – State of PA)

**Ed Samuel**                                                                                         esamuel@samnovainc.com

## AWARDS

- Employee of the Year, 2012, Samuel and Jones Securities
- Five (5) Spot Awards for Excellence, Society for College Financial Management

## PROFESSIONAL DEVELOPMENT

- Conflict Management, Smith Conflict Learning Center, MA
- Managing Personal Growth, Blessing and Smith, NJ
- Advanced Leadership and Decision Making, General Electric, PA
- High Performance Teams, Blessing and Smith, NJ

## TECHNICAL SKILLS

Advanced Excel, Oracle Financials, ACT, Saleforce.com, Hyperion, PowerCampus

## PROFESSIONAL ORGANIZATIONS

SEC Compliance Association, Philadelphia Chapter, Vice President of Membership
Pennsylvania Institute of Certified Public Accountants

## VOLUNTEER and COMMUNITY

Breakfast Mission, Wilmington, DE
Autism Foundation, Philadelphia, PA, annual fund raiser leader

# Optimizing Your Resume

# Chapter 20
# Ultimate DOs and DON'Ts

*"In any moment of decision, the best thing you can do is the right thing. The worst thing you can do is nothing."*
Theodore Roosevelt

Overall, we covered a series of principles to be applied to each section of a resume. But I also thought it would be helpful to summarize what some of the over-arching principles or "DOs" and "DON'Ts" are as we wrap up the book. They are not listed in a priority order since they are all number one!

## Ultimate DOs and DON'Ts

1. Never limit your resume to one or two pages if it does not make sense to do so.

2. Always reflect no less than your last 20 years in detail on the resume.

3. Never hide Early Career even if you summarize only the job and firm name.

4. Never NOT have a Title at the top of your resume.

Optimizing Your Resume

5. Never reduce the font size or increase the margins to accommodate getting words on a page. Make the resume easy to read in print.

6. Avoid creating a DENSE resume; use white space with your Accomplishments.

7. Make it easy for decision makers to know who you are and do not put the onus on them to figure things out.

8. Never show a disproportionate amount of accomplishments based on the number of months or years in a job.

9. Never let a firm define the actual job title your work aligns with in the industry; use a title common to the marketplace

10. Your value is never found in a job description, an activity, education or certification until you can quantify it in terms of $, #, % in some form.

11. Never begin and end with an award as an accomplishment. Put awards where they belong and speak to what you did to earn the award as the accomplishment.

12. Write the resume as if it was a storyline about the best of what you have done and then use it as a script for the interview.

13. Always add your Volunteer or Community work at the end of your resume.

Ed Samuel

# Resources and Obtaining a Word Resume Template

If you would like to obtain an online Word resume template, please send the following information to:
resume@samnovainc.com

- First and Last Name
- Phone Number (cell or home)
- Current Job Title
- Industry
- City and State
- When and where you bought this book
- Optional: state your biggest career or job challenge at hand
- Optional: attach your current resume
- Optional: if you would like help with your resume, please indicate this and one of our resume writers on our team will contact you.

If you supply us with the above information, we will gladly send our Word resume template to you. This template is to **ONLY be used by you.** Any use of our template with others is prohibited.

We offer resume services, career coaching, assessment and job search services in the Mid-Atlantic region and across the USA in the following areas:

Optimizing Your Resume

- Career Optimization
- Career Assessments and Consultations
- Resume Writing
- LinkedIn Profiles and Branding
- Building and Leveraging Formal Networks
- Job Search Strategies
- Compensation Analysis
- Targeted Job Searches
- Reverse Recruiting
- DiSC Personality Assessments
- Interview Preparation
- Job Offer Negotiation
- Post Job Offer Executive Coaching
- Rainmaking for Small Businesses and Consultants

Please reach out to Ed Samuel at esamuel@samnovainc.com, call our main number: 610-274-8214 or visit our website at www.samnovainc.com. We offer free initial consultations. Feel free to connect with Ed on LinkedIn: (Google: Ed Samuel, Career Coach, LinkedIn)

Thank you for reading this book and God bless!

## ABOUT THE AUTHOR

**Ed Samuel** is a senior Executive Career Coach, Life Coach, Resume Writer, Speaker, Rainmaker and Certified Career Assessment and Consultant Team Leader for a firm he founded, SamNova, Inc. (www.samnovainc.com). His office is based in Kennett Square, PA.

Ed's team provides comprehensive resume writing services, LinkedIn profiles and branding, formal network building, job search strategies, targeted job searches, interview coaching, career assessments, personality tests and retirement coaching. His emphasis is to support mid- to senior-level executives across multiple functional roles, industries and locations across the USA. He also supports early stage college graduates.

He has three hundred plus documented testimonials of which more than one hundred and ten are posted on LinkedIn.

Ed has written and improved hundreds of resumes resulting in positive outcomes for his clients. He has led more than one hundred and fifty executive networking forums with thousands of attendees over the last twelve years. He leads the monthly Career Professionals Executive Networking Group (CPENG) forum in Newark, DE and monthly Cross Talks forum of emerging small business owners and consultants in Glen Mills, PA. Ed leads a virtual team of twenty-six Career Assessment Consultants across the region and beyond. Ed hosts a bi-weekly Philadelphia radio program called, "Optimize Your Career" on Saturday mornings: https://www.1180wfyl.com/.

Optimizing Your Resume

He is a frequent speaker at: ExecuNet, TPNG, Chem/Pharma, Joseph's People, Lehigh Valley Professionals, Financial Executives Networking Group, Technical Professionals Networking Group, Delaware Chamber of Commerce, Cross Talks, Newtown Networking Forum and more. Ed is also very active in Believers in Business in the greater King of Prussia, PA area.

Ed has thirty years of corporate experience in human resources, finance and global operations with various sized companies, from multi-billion-dollar firms to emerging start-ups. He has been a third-party recruiter with depth in consulting, contingency and retained searches. Ed has also led a corporate recruiting team for a $1B division of a medical device firm.

Ed also has a private non-profit foundation concerning stewardship redemption and is a US leader for Crown Financial Ministries.

Made in the
USA
Lexington, KY